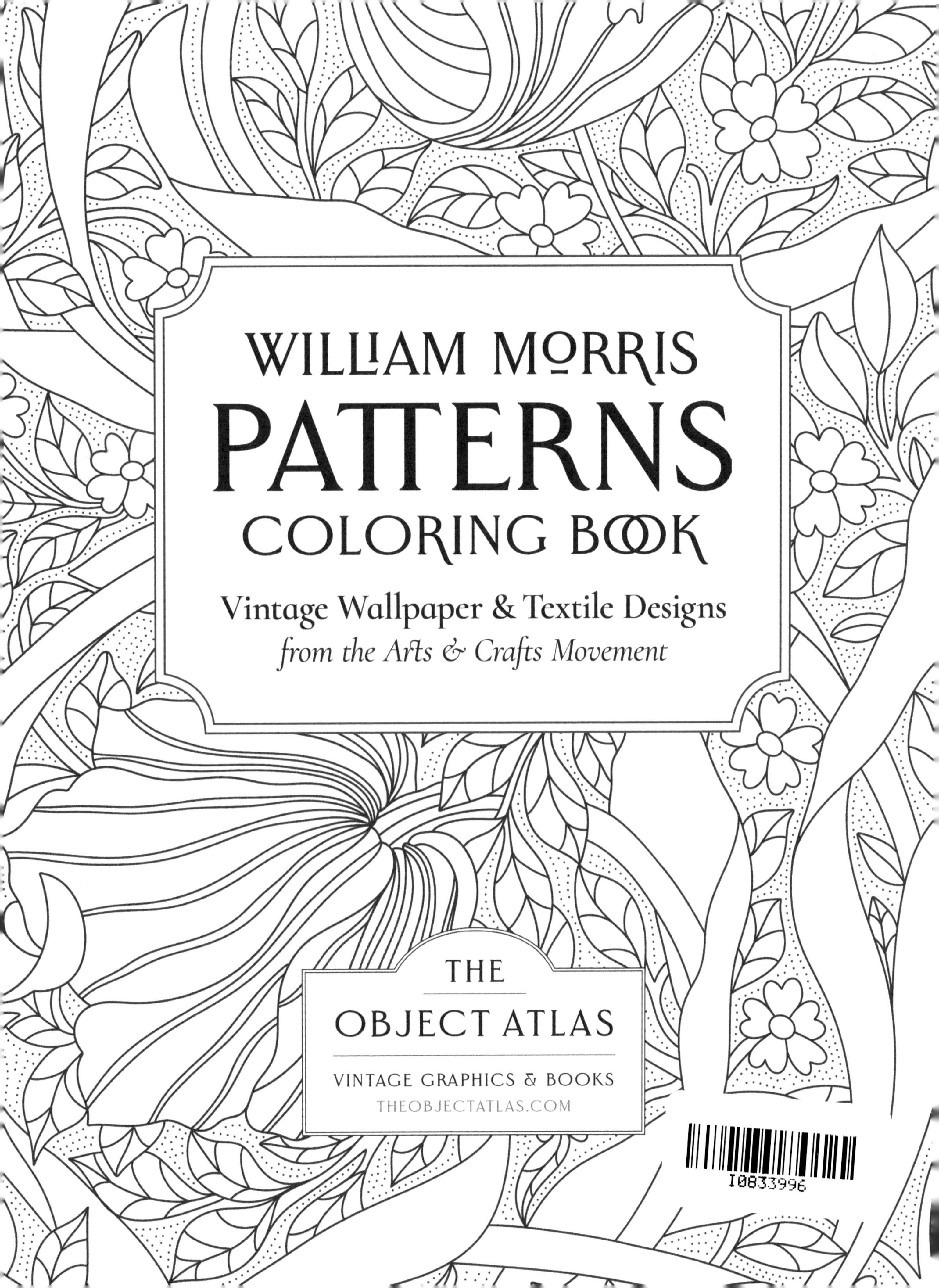

WILLIAM MORRIS PATTERNS COLORING BOOK

Vintage Wallpaper & Textile Designs
from the Arts & Crafts Movement

THE
OBJECT ATLAS
VINTAGE GRAPHICS & BOOKS
THEOBJECTATLAS.COM

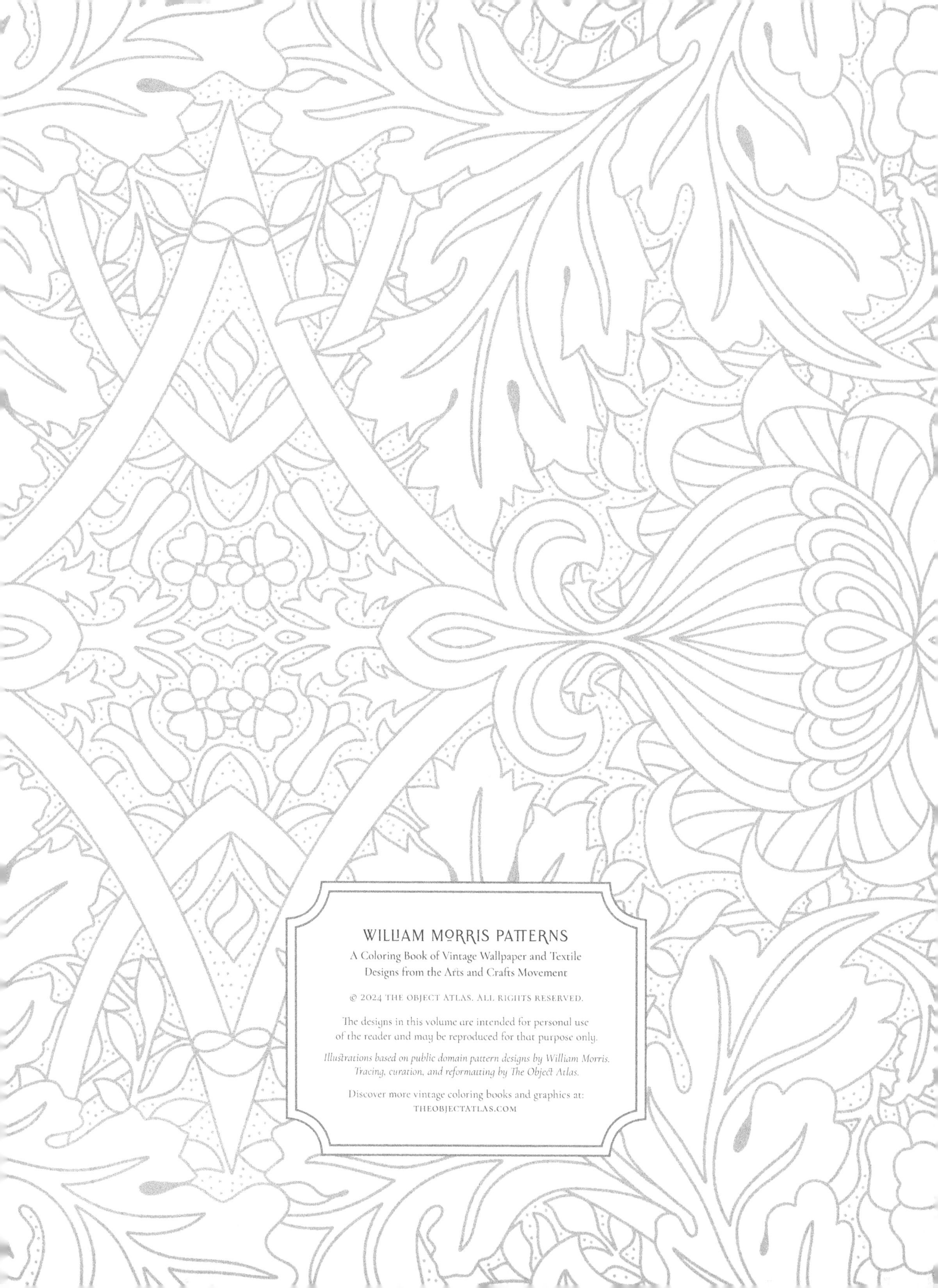

WILLIAM MORRIS PATTERNS

A Coloring Book of Vintage Wallpaper and Textile Designs from the Arts and Crafts Movement

Illustrations based on public domain pattern designs by William Morris. Tracing, curation, and reformatting by The Object Atlas.

Discover more vintage coloring books and graphics at:
THEOBJECTATLAS.COM

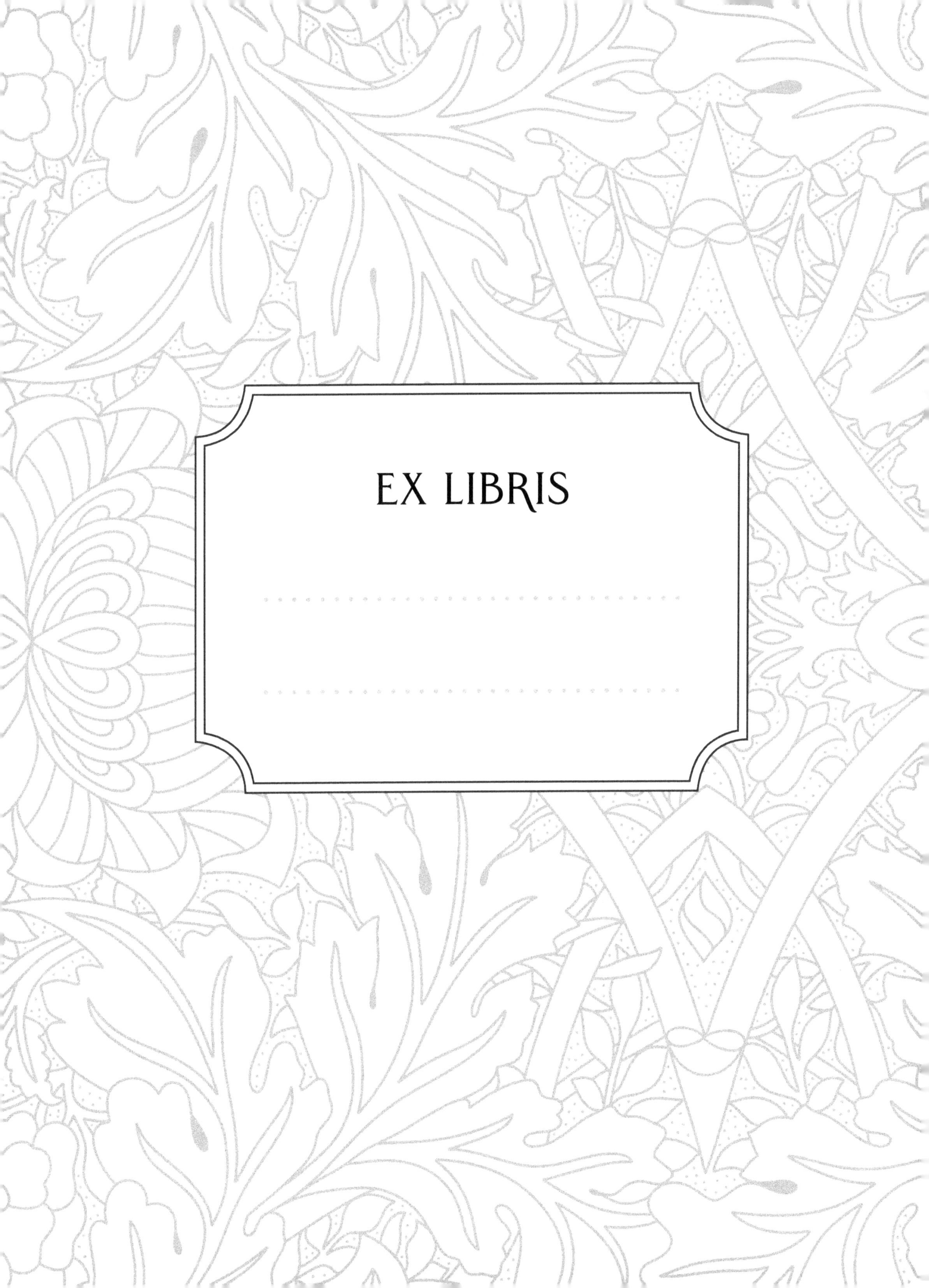
EX LIBRIS

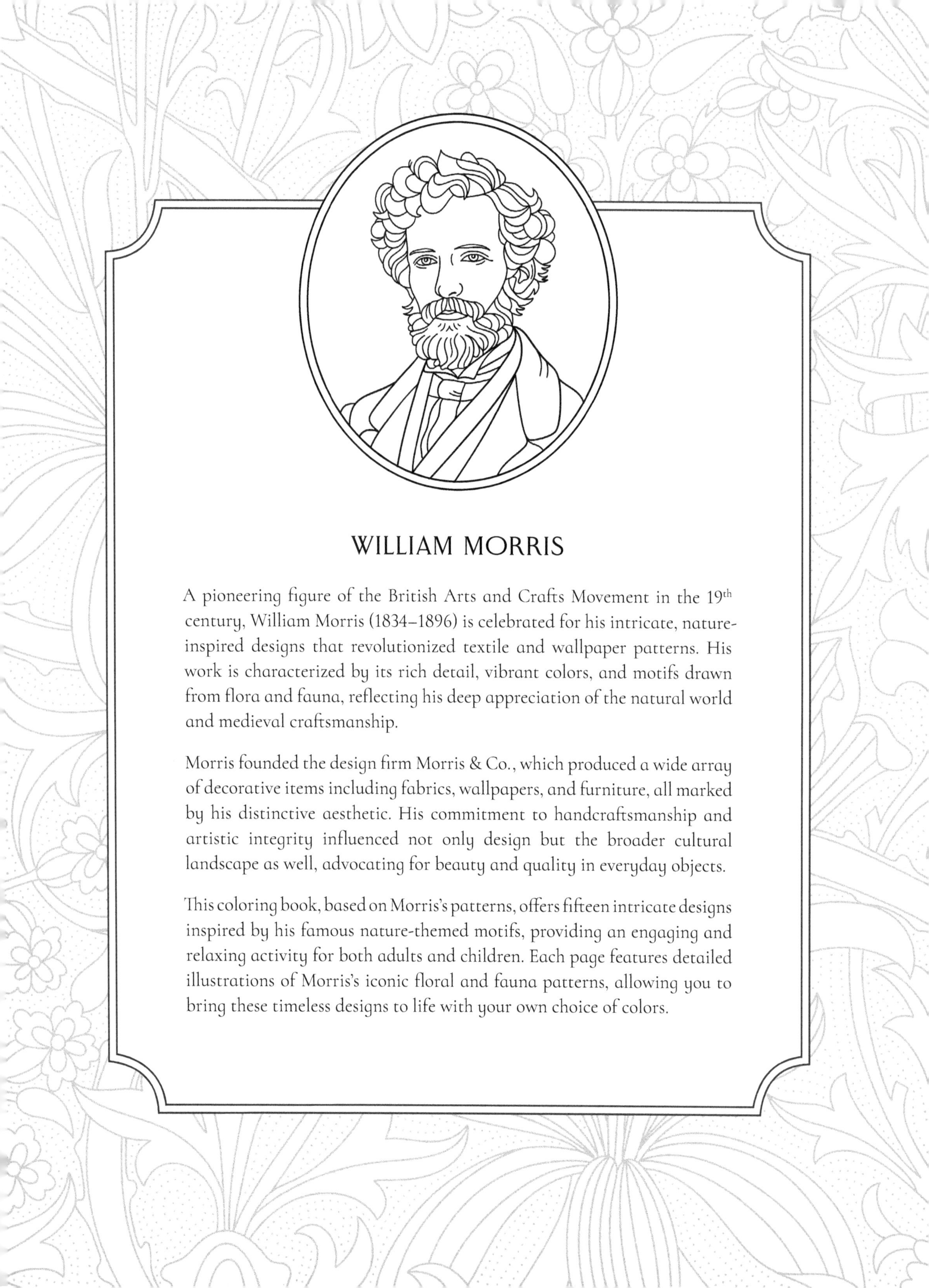

WILLIAM MORRIS

A pioneering figure of the British Arts and Crafts Movement in the 19th century, William Morris (1834–1896) is celebrated for his intricate, nature-inspired designs that revolutionized textile and wallpaper patterns. His work is characterized by its rich detail, vibrant colors, and motifs drawn from flora and fauna, reflecting his deep appreciation of the natural world and medieval craftsmanship.

Morris founded the design firm Morris & Co., which produced a wide array of decorative items including fabrics, wallpapers, and furniture, all marked by his distinctive aesthetic. His commitment to handcraftsmanship and artistic integrity influenced not only design but the broader cultural landscape as well, advocating for beauty and quality in everyday objects.

This coloring book, based on Morris's patterns, offers fifteen intricate designs inspired by his famous nature-themed motifs, providing an engaging and relaxing activity for both adults and children. Each page features detailed illustrations of Morris's iconic floral and fauna patterns, allowing you to bring these timeless designs to life with your own choice of colors.

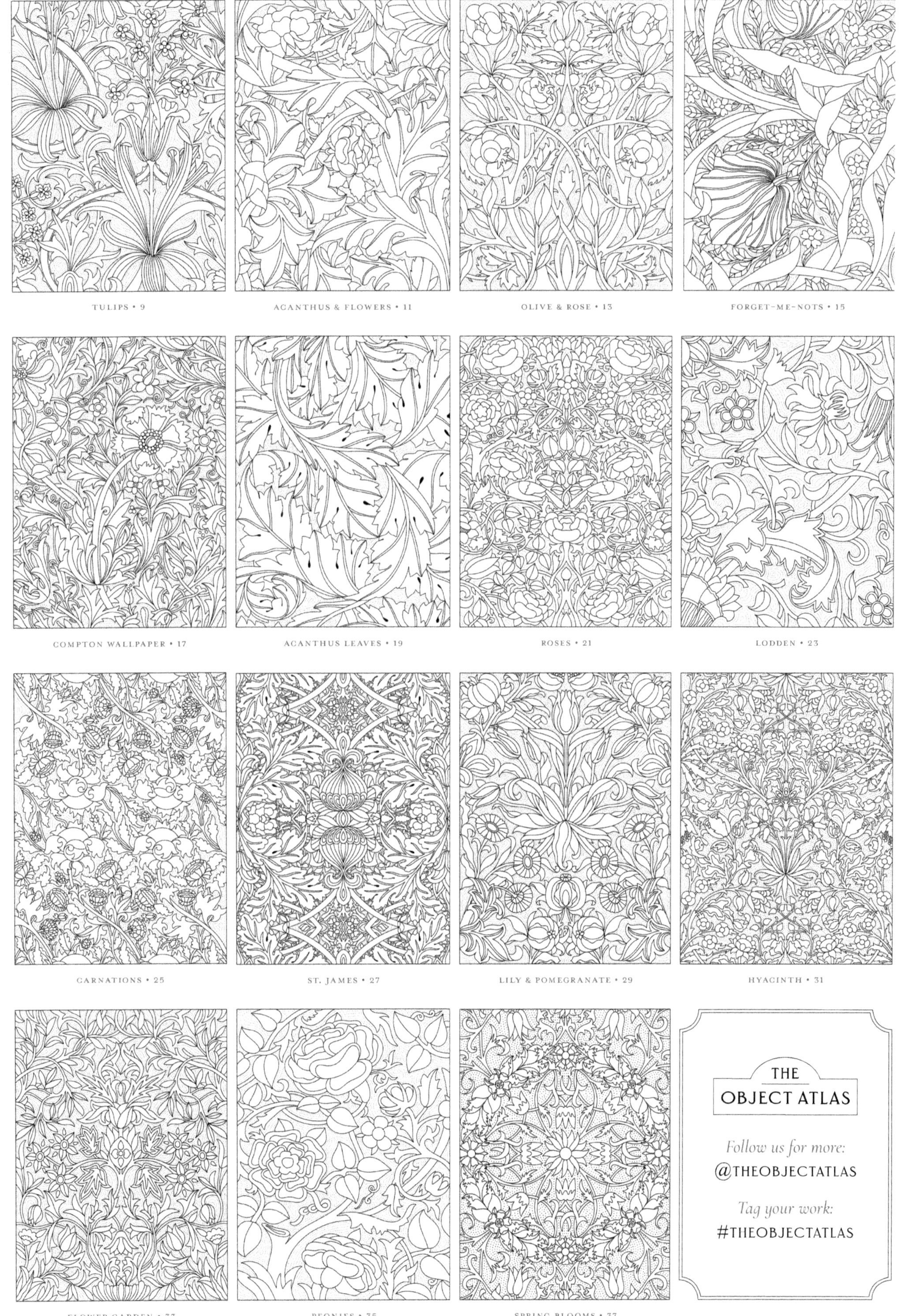
THE
OBJECT ATLAS
Follow us for more:
@THEOBJECTATLAS
Tag your work:
#THEOBJECTATLAS

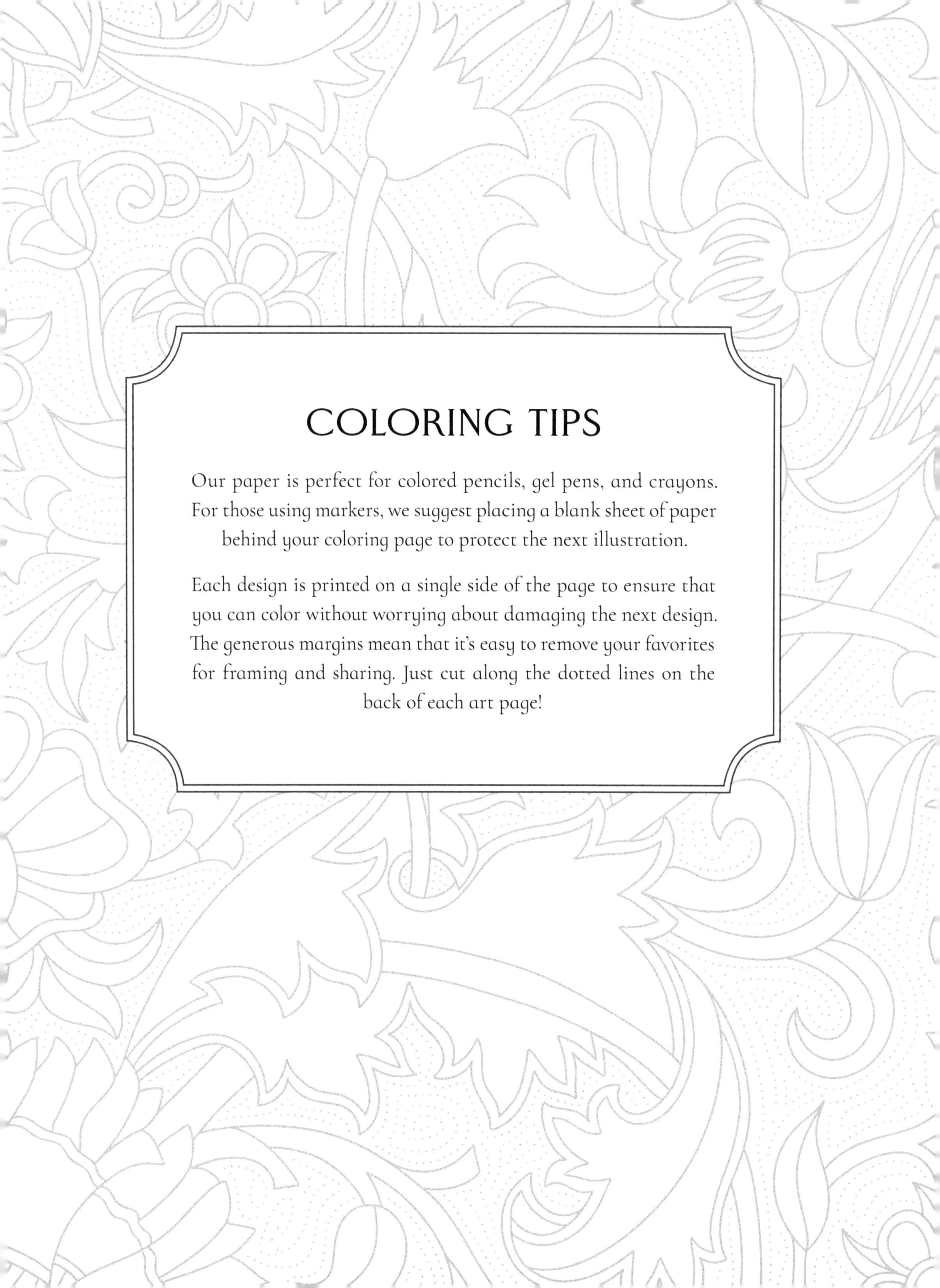

COLORING TIPS

Our paper is perfect for colored pencils, gel pens, and crayons. For those using markers, we suggest placing a blank sheet of paper behind your coloring page to protect the next illustration.

Each design is printed on a single side of the page to ensure that you can color without worrying about damaging the next design. The generous margins mean that it's easy to remove your favorites for framing and sharing. Just cut along the dotted lines on the back of each art page!

SWATCH PALETTE

Sample, test, and combine colors

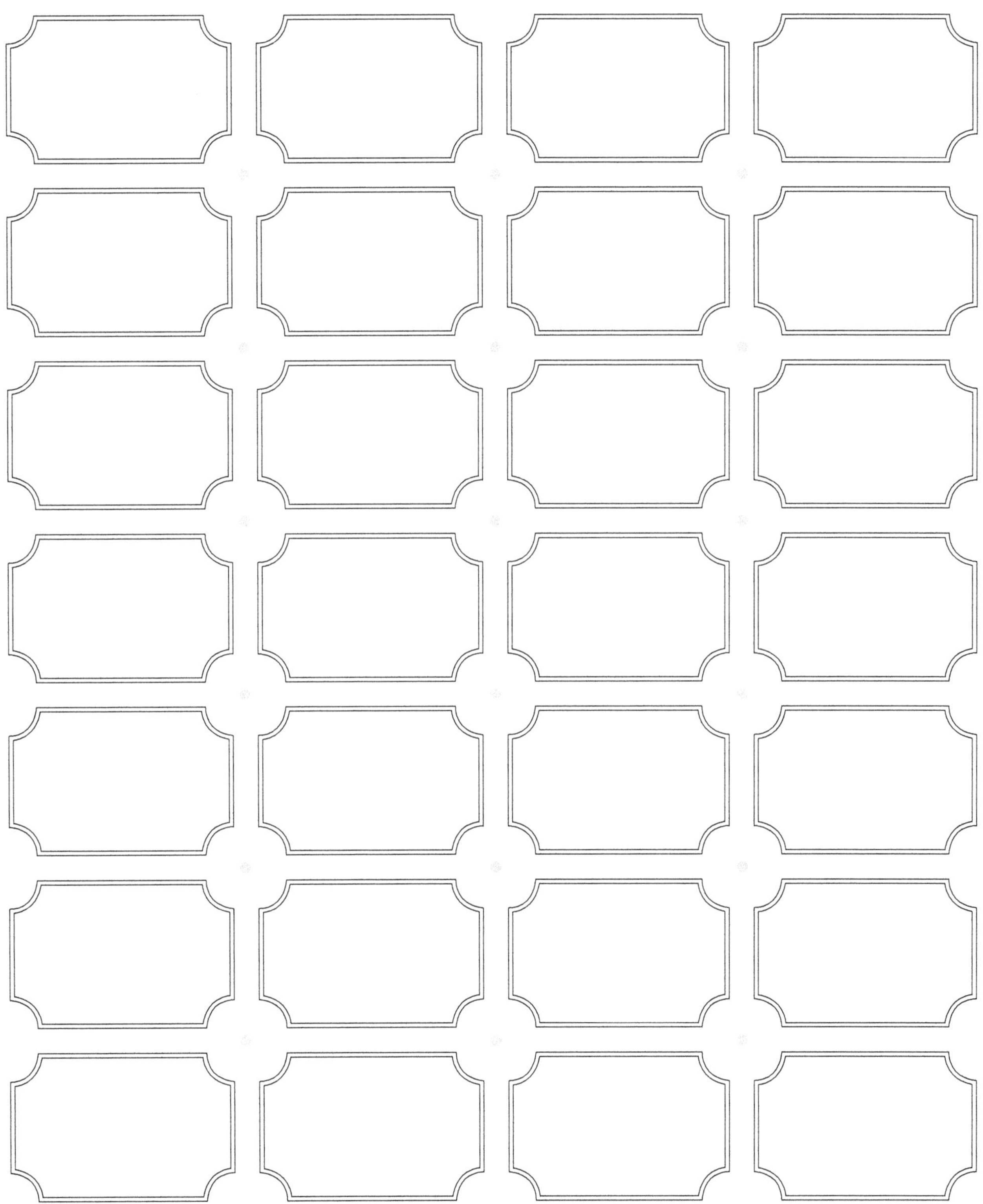

TULIPS

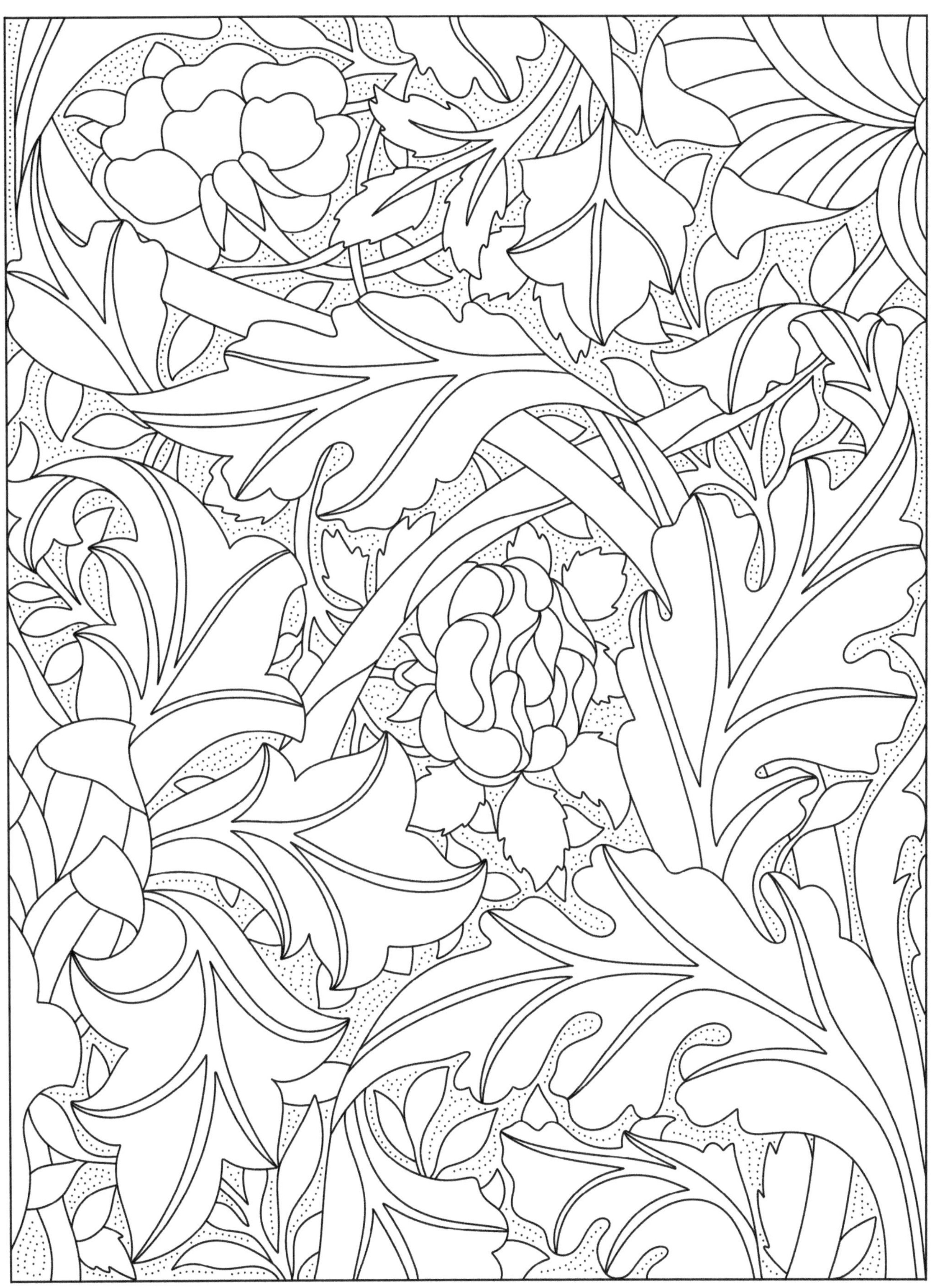

ACANTHUS & FLOWERS

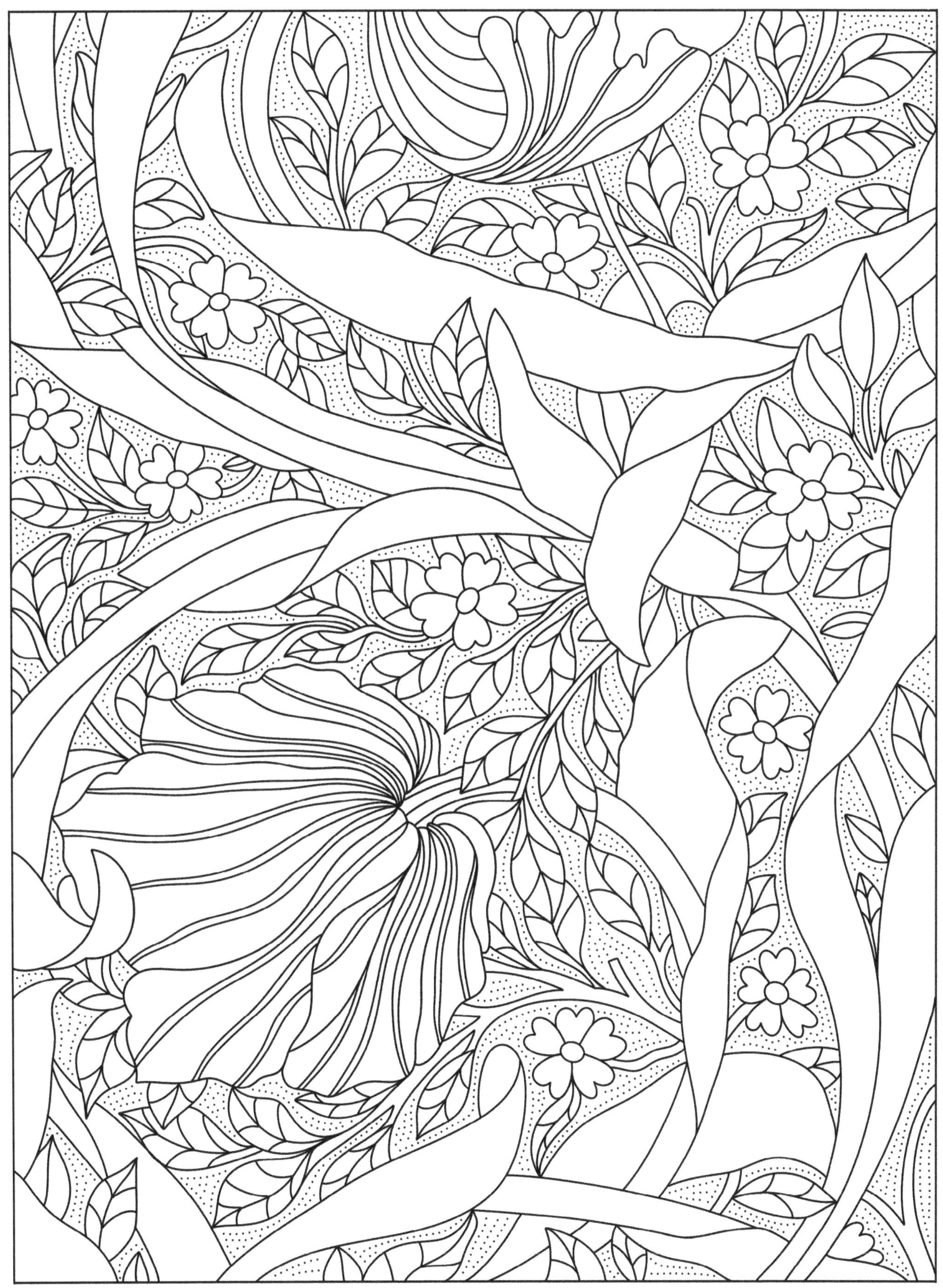

FORGET-ME-NOTS

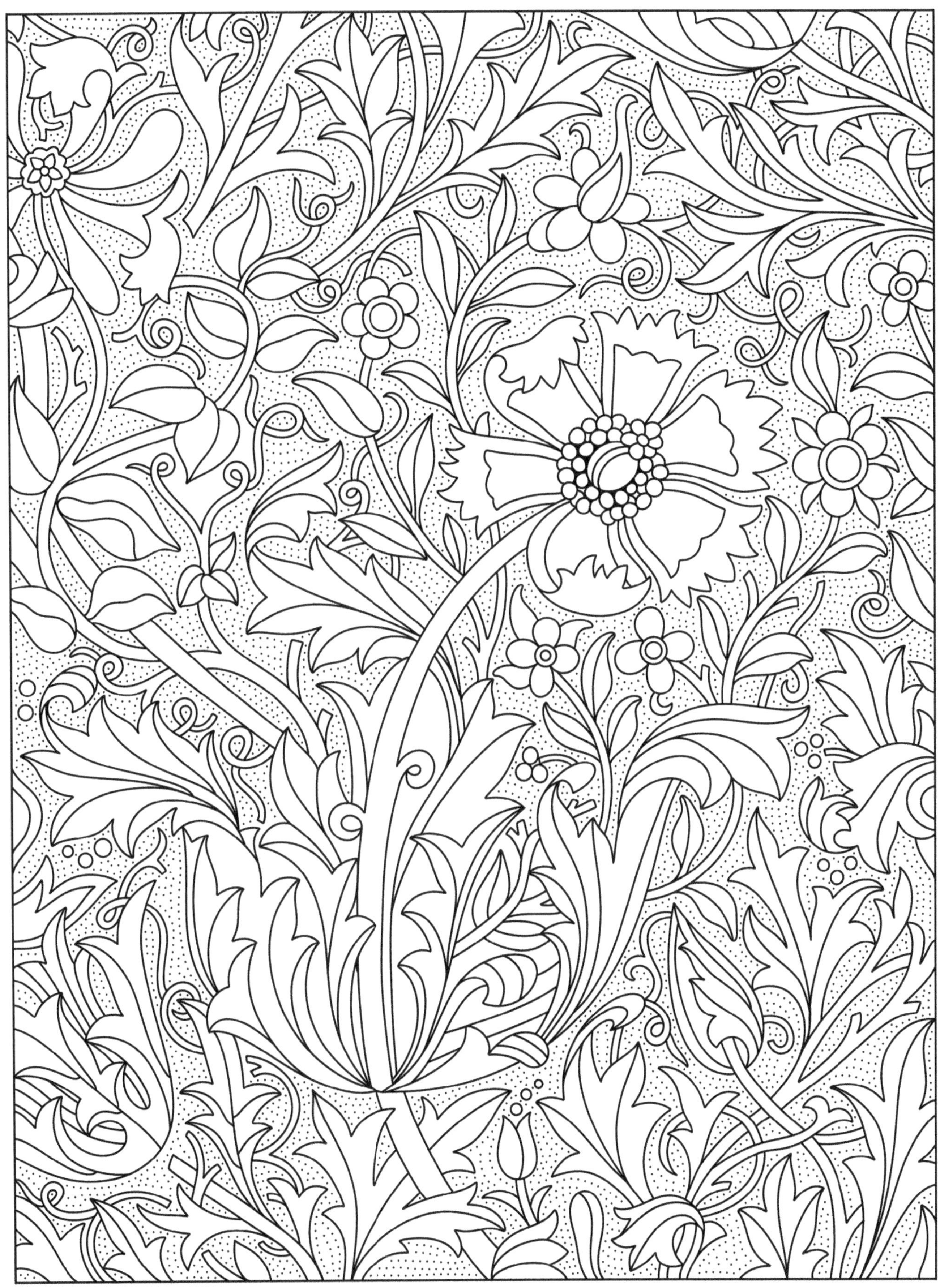

COMPTON WALLPAPER

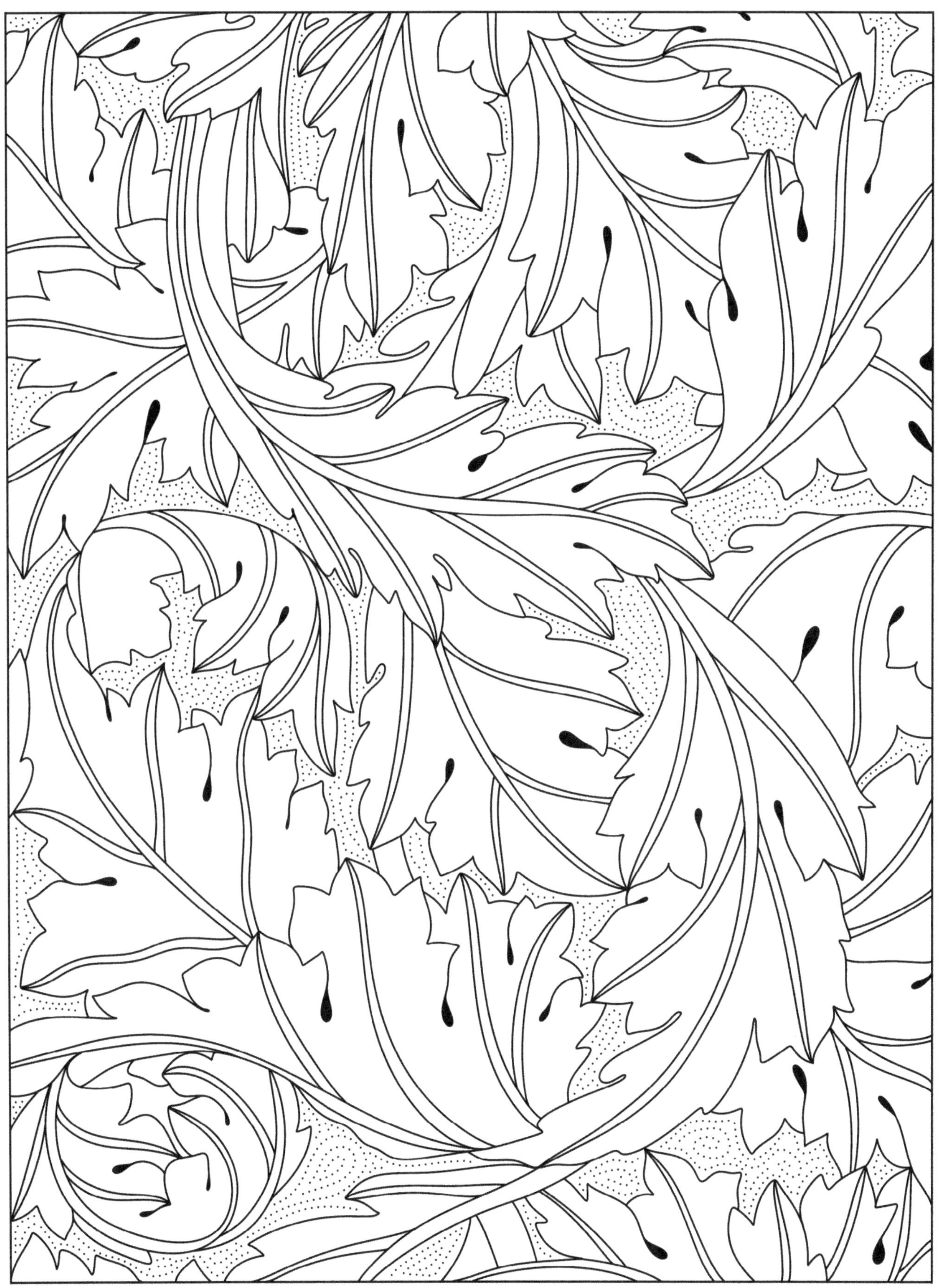

ACANTHUS LEAVES

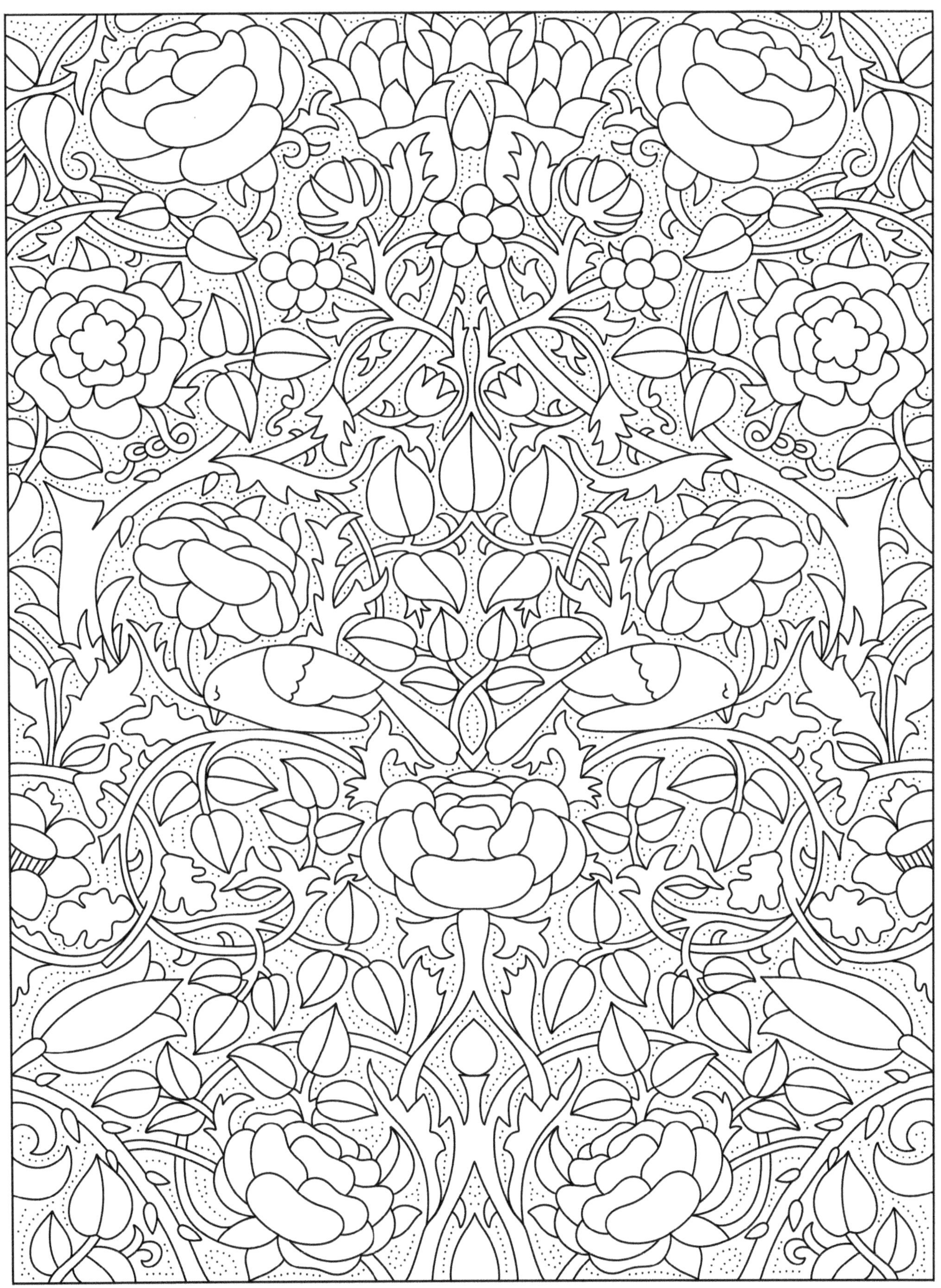

ROSES

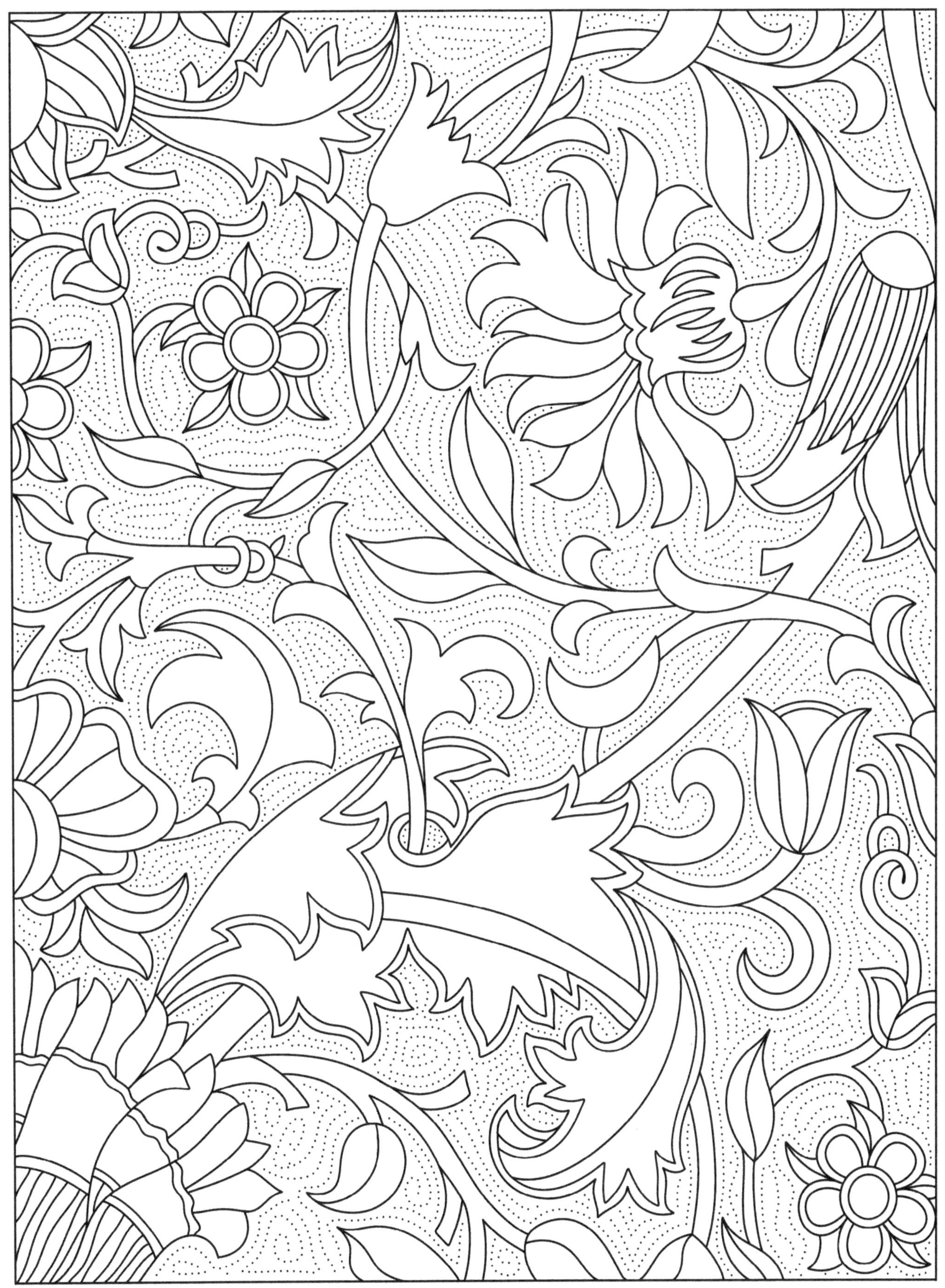

LODDEN

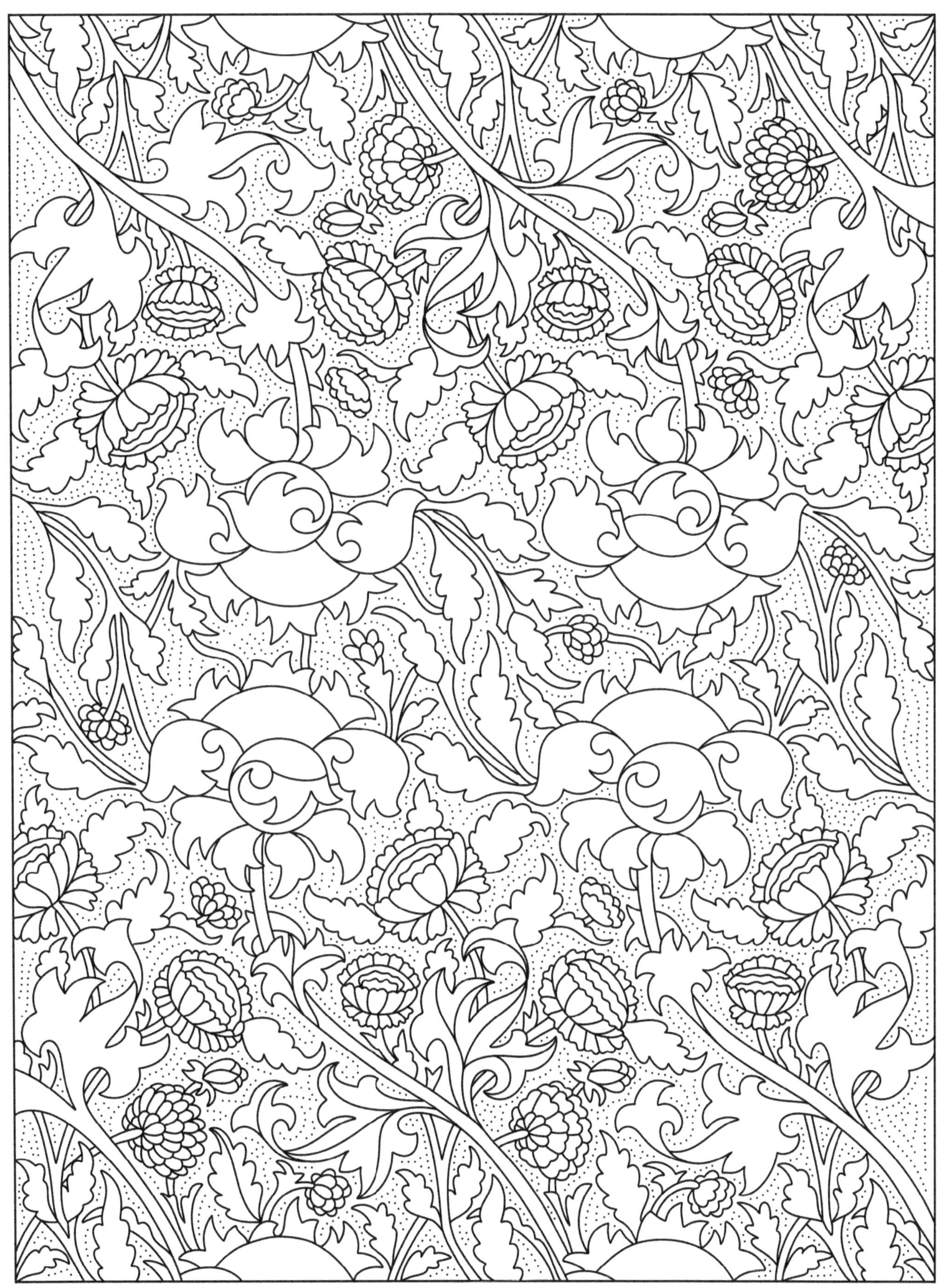

CARNATIONS

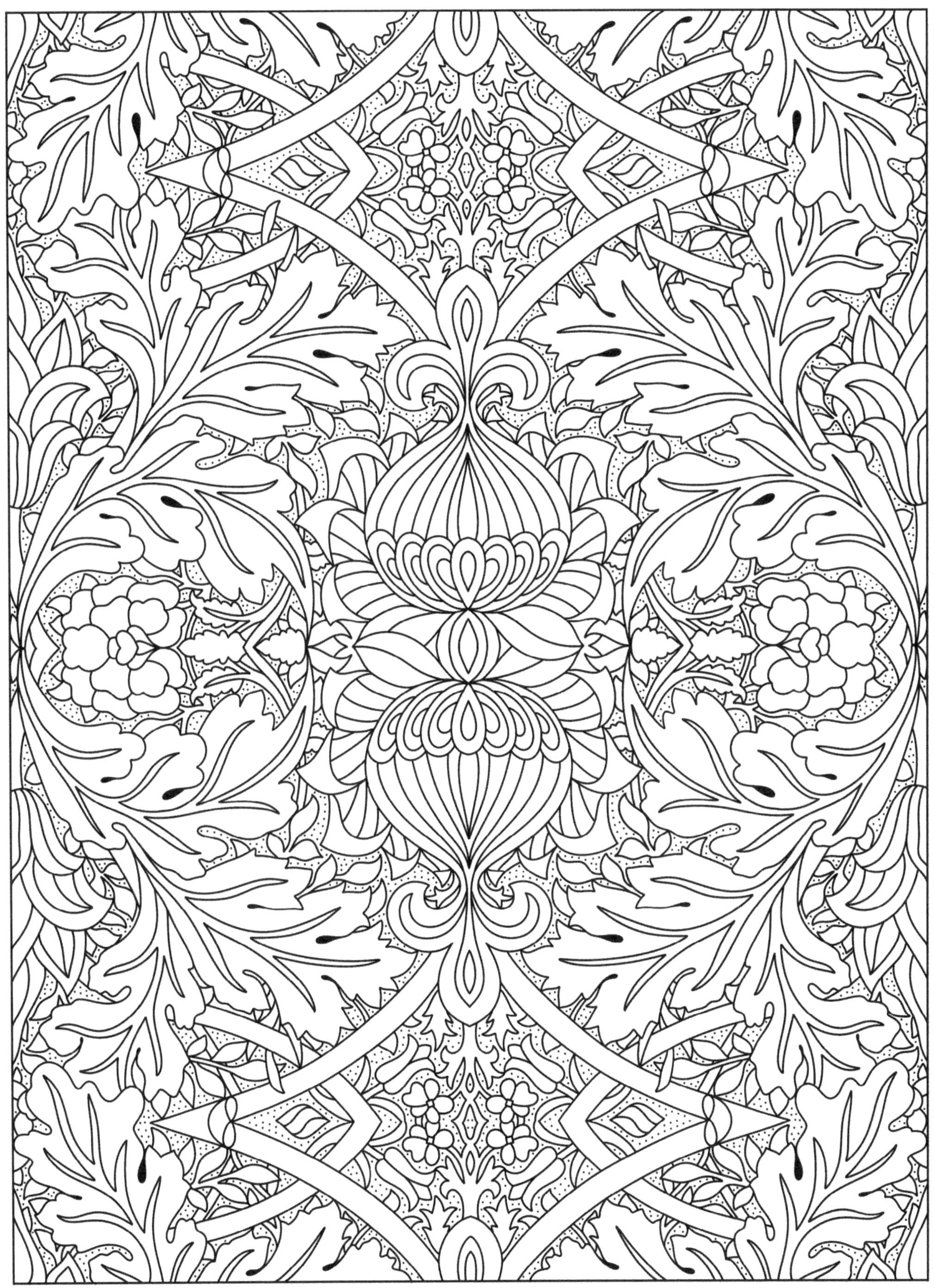

ST. JAMES

LILY & POMEGRANATE

30

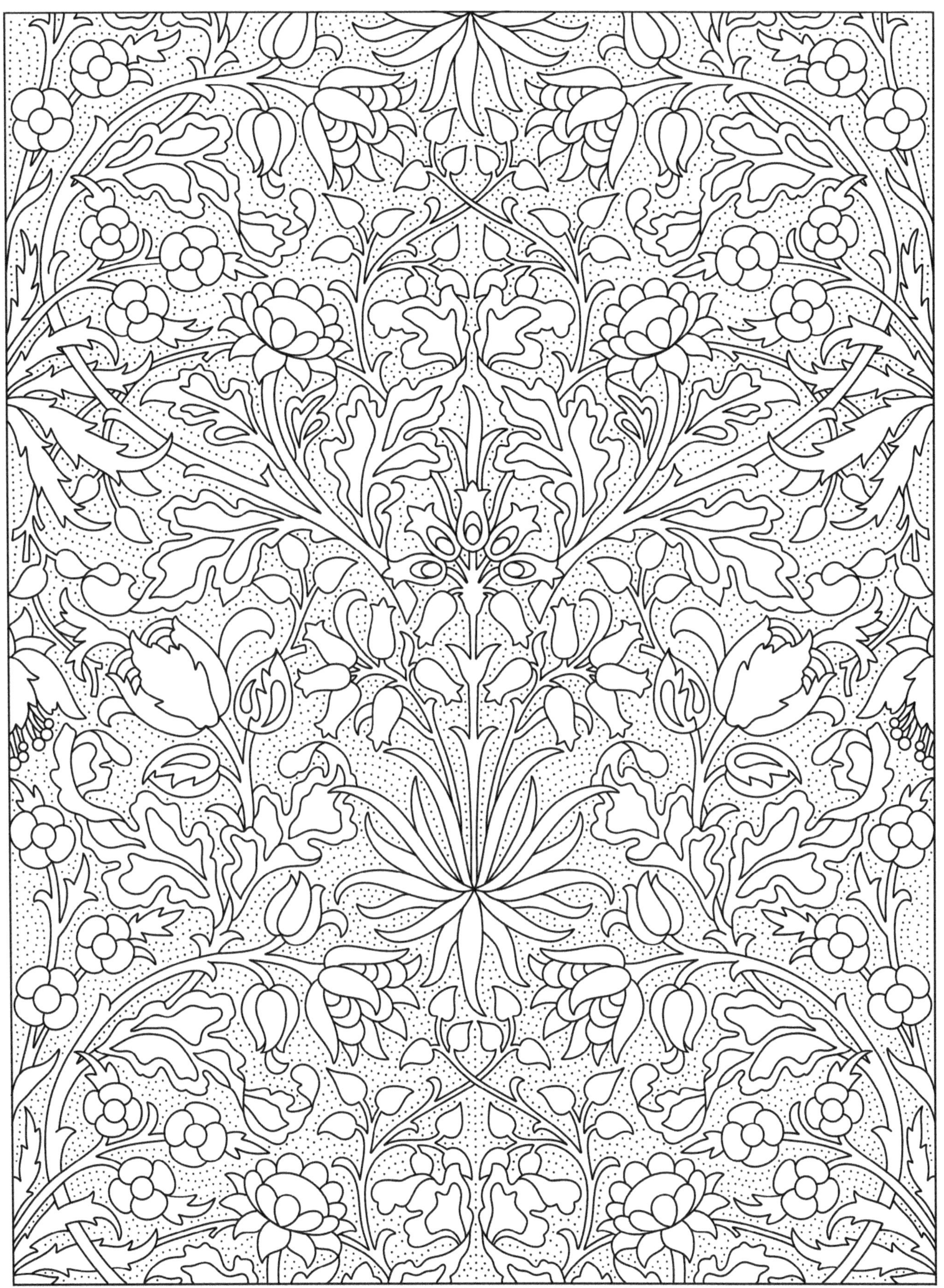

HYACINTH

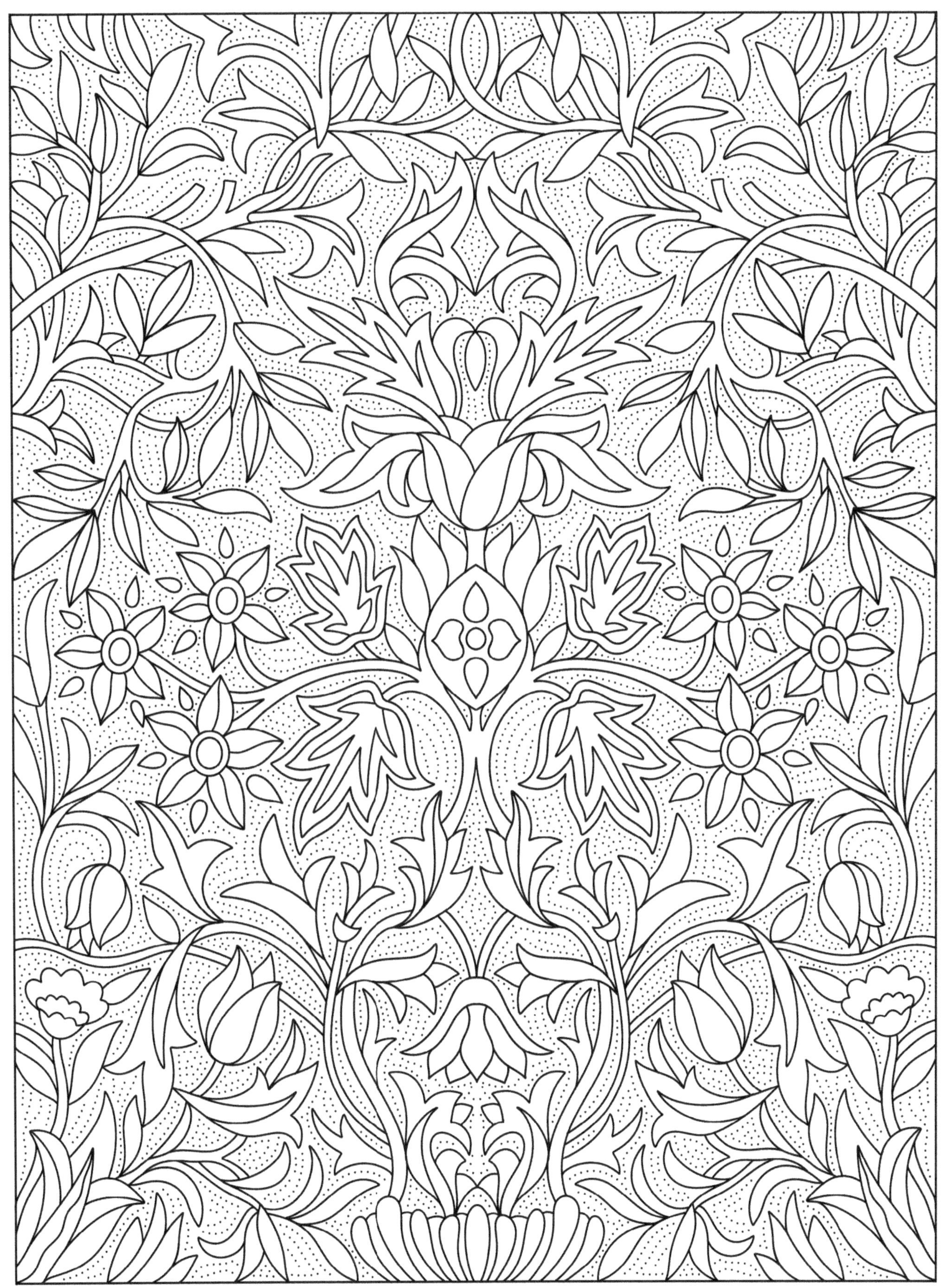

FLOWER GARDEN

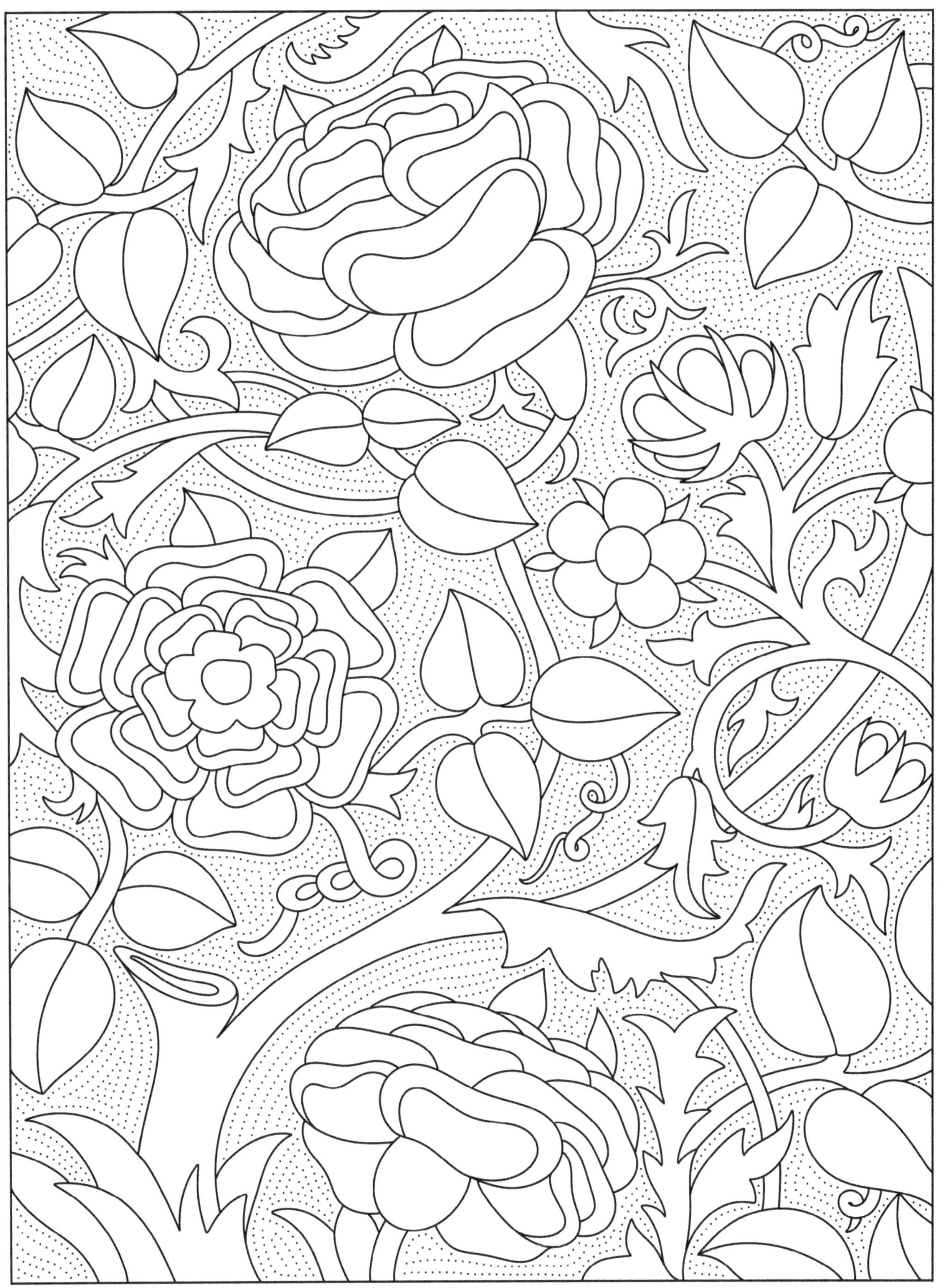

PEONIES

SPRING BLOOMS

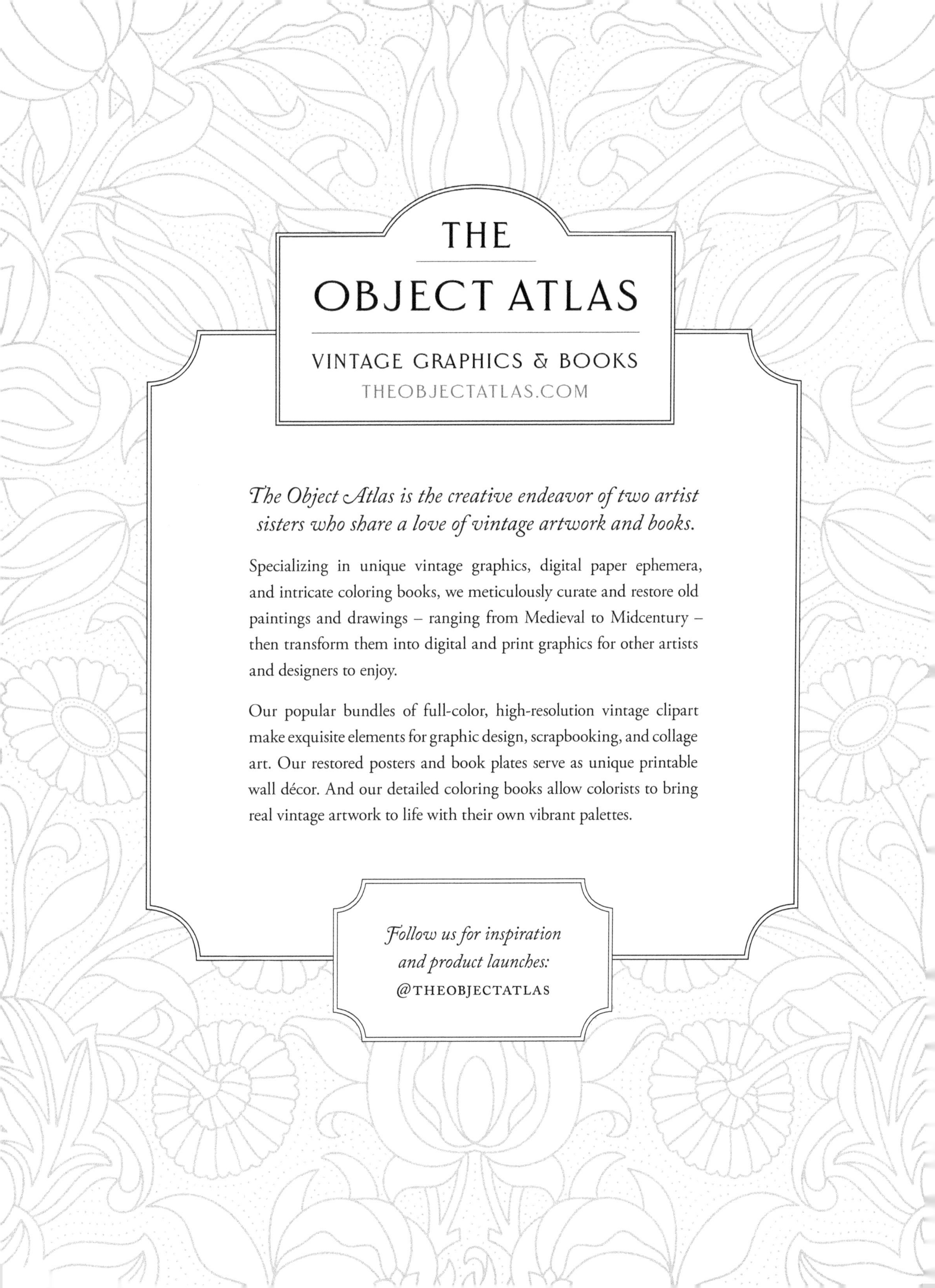

THE OBJECT ATLAS

VINTAGE GRAPHICS & BOOKS

THEOBJECTATLAS.COM

The Object Atlas is the creative endeavor of two artist sisters who share a love of vintage artwork and books.

Specializing in unique vintage graphics, digital paper ephemera, and intricate coloring books, we meticulously curate and restore old paintings and drawings – ranging from Medieval to Midcentury – then transform them into digital and print graphics for other artists and designers to enjoy.

Our popular bundles of full-color, high-resolution vintage clipart make exquisite elements for graphic design, scrapbooking, and collage art. Our restored posters and book plates serve as unique printable wall décor. And our detailed coloring books allow colorists to bring real vintage artwork to life with their own vibrant palettes.

Follow us for inspiration and product launches:

@THEOBJECTATLAS

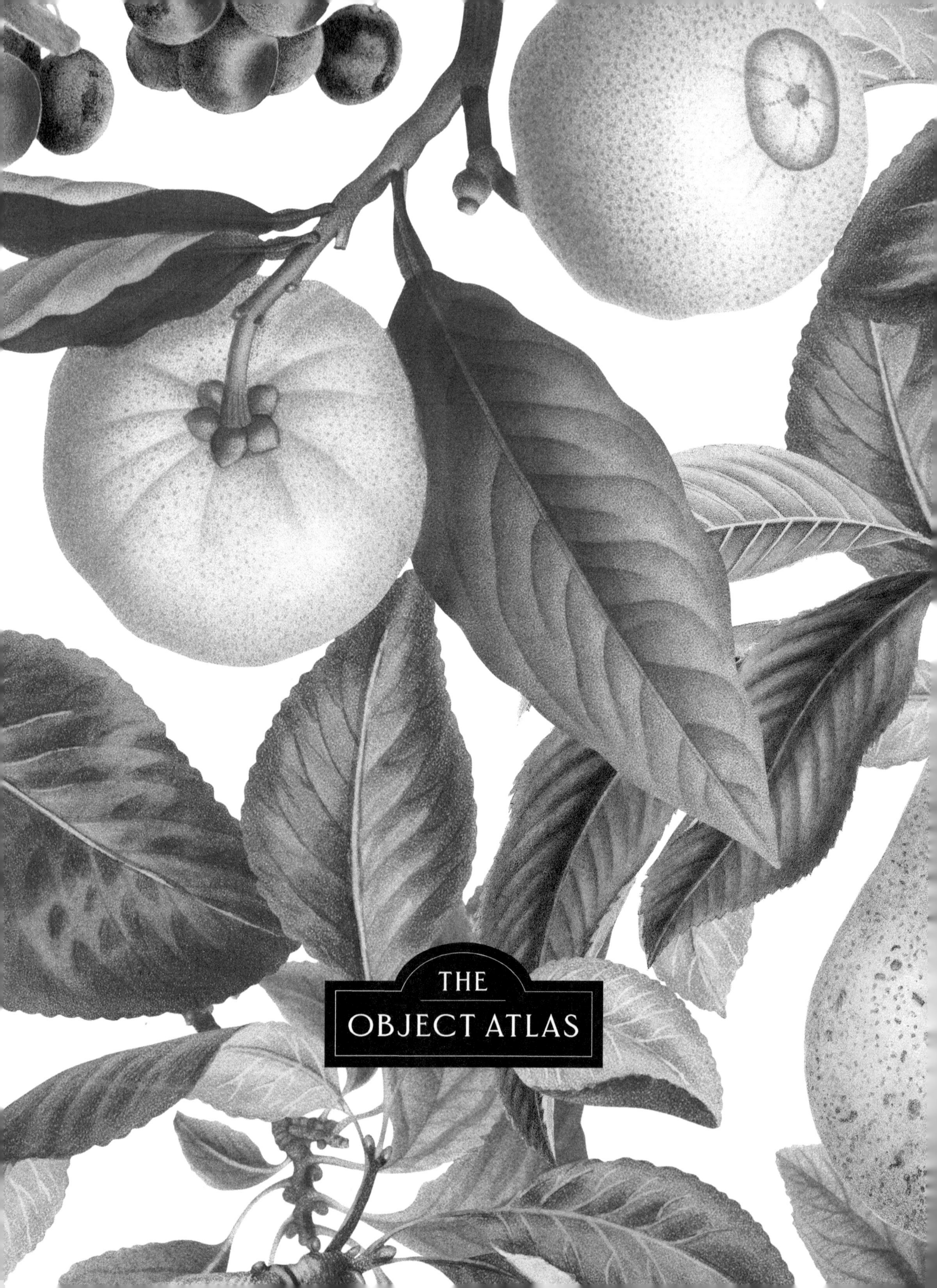
THE
OBJECT ATLAS

www.ingramcontent.com/pod-product-compliance
Lightning Source LLC
LaVergne TN
LVHW081255100826
845148LV00009B/1224

9798987193631